Table of Contents

Table of Contents

About the Author

Having loved football for over 40 years I have always been interested in the History of the game. Despite not being a Newcastle United fan, I have always had huge admiration for the club and their fanbase. Some of their players will go down as my favorites of all time.

For me Alan Shearer is the greatest striker English football has ever seen. I have heard arguments from other fans of other clubs for their man. But no one will compare with Super Al for me.

The Kevin Keegan era still resonates with me from the danger of relegation to the third tier to a title race and taking on Sir Alex Ferguson never taking a backwards step.

From the swagger of Ginola to the chip of Albert against Schmeichel the early Premier League years and my formative years as a football fan has Newcastle stamped all over it

My love of history and fondness of the club led me to write this quizbook. I will read and learn as I go. And I hope I can do this great club some justice.

Howay the lads!

This is the Newcastle United Quizbook

The Quizbook is intended to take you through the History of Newcastle United Football Club. (Everything is correct at date of writing 2023)

It starts with the early years and will follow a rough chronology through to the present day. The early questions are naturally harder – but oh so important to understand the importance of the history of Newcastle United.

The book includes sections of multiple-choice questions in blocks of 10. In between the multiple-choice questions there are a variety of other questions I have put together in slightly different formats.

You will be asked to name the player, name those that crossed the divide, remember as many players as possible in some of Newcastle's biggest matches. Some of them will take time and need to be thought about. If you take time to test your memory you will be rewarded

Each section can be cross referenced against the answers provided towards the end of the book.

Grab a drink, something to eat and a pencil and enjoy the quizbook – or take it to your friends and fill out together – or quiz your best mate who claims to know everything about Newcastle and see how much they truly know.

Most of all – enjoy and remember the history and traditions of this great club.

B Demure

Newcastle United Quizbook

The Early History of Newcastle United

1. On 9th December 1892 Newcastle United was officially borne. What was the name of the club prior to this?

    a. Newcastle Rovers ☐

    b. Newcastle East End ☐

    c. Newcastle West End ☐

    d. Newcastle City ☐

2. Who were Newcastle United's first opponents in the second division in the 1893-4 season?

    a. Woolwich Arsenal ☐

    b. Liverpool ☐

    c. West Bromwich Albion ☐

    d. Doncaster Rovers ☐

3. In 1898-99 Newcastle United played their first game in the first division of English football. What position did they finish?

    a. 5th ☐

    b. 7th ☐

    c. 13th ☐

    d. 18th ☐

4. What year did Newcastle win their first ever top division title?

    a. 1899-1900 ☐

    b. 1900-1901 ☐

    c. 1902-1903 ☐

    d. 1904-1905 ☐

5. In total how many titles did Newcastle United win between 1900-1910?

    a. 1 ☐

    b. 2 ☐

    c. 3 ☐

    d. 4 ☐

6. Who was the Newcastle United manager from 1895 until 1930?

    a. Barry Coates ☐

    b. Steve Chalmers ☐

    c. Frank Watt ☐

    d. Malcolm Archer ☐

7. In 1904 a Goalkeeper made his debut for the club. He went on to make 496 appearances and is still the leading appearance maker who is he?

    a. Tommy Langthorne ☐

    b. James Carney ☐

    c. Frank Hudspeth ☐

    d. Jimmy Lawrence ☐

8. Newcastle first won the FA Cup trophy in 1909-1910 – who were their opponents?

    a. Manchester United ☐

    b. Barnsley ☐

    c. Liverpool ☐

    d. Woolwich Arsenal ☐

9. The 1909-10 final went to a replay after a 1-1 draw. The replay finished 2-0 Who scored both goals?

    a. Jock Rutherford ☐

    b. Vic Watson ☐

    c. Albert Shepherd ☐

    d. Hughie Gallacher ☐

10. Newcastle reached the FA cup final again in 1910-1911. Unfortunately losing 1-0 in a replay – who were their opponents?

    a. Bradford City ☐

    b. Manchester United ☐

    c. Barnsley ☐

    d. West Ham United ☐

(ANSWERS CAN BE FOUND ON PAGE 75)

SECTION TWO

NAME THE FAMOUS MAGPIES

1. Signed for a fee of £1.75 million from Bristol City in 1993 this player scored 68 goals in 84 matches for the club before leaving for around 7 million in 1995

   _____

2 Played 337 league games from the club between 1982 and 1992 scoring 14 goals the versatile defender was an Irish international.

   _____

3   Spent his whole career at Newcastle between 1945 and 1957. He scored 201 goals in 399 games and won three FA Cups with the club

┌───┐
│   │
│   │
└───┘

4   A Newcastle youth player who was released and started his career with Carlisle United in 1979. He returned to Newcastle in 1983 scoring 61 goals in 164 games before leaving to join Liverpool. He returned to the northeast in 1993 and scored 58 in 162 games

┌───┐
│   │
│   │
└───┘

5   Signed from Bury in 1973. This player also had two spells at the club – joining Liverpool in between. With 169 games and 24 goals across both spells this player also returned in a coaching capacity between 92-98 and 05-08.

┌───┐
│   │
│   │
└───┘

6 A Peruvian set piece specialist signed from Boca Juniors for £2.5 million. He scored 48 goals in just over 300 games across two spells for the club

7 Born in Sunderland this striker scored 82 goals in 206 league games and was vitally important in the 1964-65 promotion winning team. He moved to West Ham for a fee of £120,000

8 138 goals in 257 Newcastle appearances signed for £180,000 from Luton Town in 1971. He left for an unusual fee of £333,333.34 to join Arsenal in 1976

9   A Senegalese international striker. Signed from West Ham for free after their relegation. He scored 29 goals in 58 games before signing for Chelsea in January 2013

```
┌─────────────────────────────────────┐
│                                     │
│                                     │
└─────────────────────────────────────┘
```

10 Irish stopper who played 462 games for Newcastle between 1997 and 2009.

```
┌─────────────────────────────────────┐
│                                     │
│                                     │
└─────────────────────────────────────┘
```

(ANSWERS CAN BE FOUND ON PAGE 76)

SECTION THREE

NEWCASTLE UNITED
1974 FA CUP FINAL XI

(The numbers used are to represent positions only – they are
not accurate as worn on the day)

How many of the Newcastle's 1974 FA CUP XI final can you name? Initials used to give you a helping hand:

1. IM	
2. FC	
3. AK	
4. TM	
5. PH	
6. BM	
7. JS	
8. TC	
9. MM	
10. JT	
11. TH	

Bonus point available. Can you name the substitute used?

12. TG	

(ANSWERS CAN BE FOUND ON PAGE 77)

SECTION FOUR

NEWCASTLE UNITED 1920s-1940s

1. On 26th April 1924 Newcastle won the FA Cup Final 2-0 who were their opponents?

    a. Aston Villa ☐

    b. West Ham United ☐

    c. Bolton Wanderers ☐

    d. Preston North End ☐

2. Newcastle were Division one winners in the 1926-27 season. Their highest scoring game this season was a 7-3 victory over which club?

    a. Liverpool ☐

    b. Everton ☐

    c. Bolton Wanderers ☐

    d. Tottenham Hotspur ☐

3. Newcastle's top scorer this season scored 39 league goals. Who was he?

    a. Stan Seymour ☐

    b. Tommy McDonald ☐

    c. Hughie Gallacher ☐

    d. Jimmy Trotter ☐

4. Newcastle recorded their largest attendance of 69,386 on 3 September 1930 against who?

    a. Sunderland ☐

    b. Chelsea ☐

    c. West Bromwich Albion ☐

    d. Cardiff City ☐

5. On 23 April 1932 Newcastle won the FA Cup in front of 92,000 at Wembley. A 2-1 win over Arsenal thanks to a brace from Jack Allen. His first goal was deemed controversial for what reason?

    a. He punched the ball into the net ☐

    b. The ball went out of play prior to the goal being scored ☐

    c. The Arsenal goalkeeper was down injured but play continued ☐

    d. Allen was clearly offside ☐

6. After 35 years in the top Division Newcastle suffered relegation. In which season did this happen?

    a. 1931-32 ☐

    b. 1932-33 ☐

    c. 1933-34 ☐

    d. 1936-37 ☐

7. In 1939 which former player was appointed Newcastle manager? He went on to have three spells as manager appointed again in 1950 and 1956

    a. Stan Seymour ☐

    b. George Martin ☐

    c. Tom Mather ☐

    d. Frank Watt ☐

8. On 5 October 1946 Newcastle achieved their record victory against Newport County. What was the final score?

    a. 6-0 ☐

    b. 10-1 ☐

    c. 13-0 ☐

    d. 15-2 ☐

9. Who scored 6 goals in this record victory against Newport County?

    a. Hughie Gallacher ☐

    b. Joe Sibley ☐

    c. Frank Brennan ☐

    d. Len Shackleton ☐

10. In the 1947-48 season Newcastle finished second in Division two gaining promotion to the top division. What club won the league?

    a. Fulham ☐

    b. Leicester City ☐

    c. Sheffield Wednesday ☐

    d. Birmingham City ☐

(ANSWERS CAN BE FOUND ON PAGE 78)

SECTION FIVE

Newcastle United 1950s-1960s

1. Newcastle won the FA Cup in the 1950-51 season. Which legendary striker scored 2 goals in the 2-0 Final Victory over Blackpool?

    a. Charlie Crowe ☐

    b. Tommy Walker ☐

    c. Bobby Mitchell ☐

    d. Jackie Milburn ☐

2. George Robledo scored 39 league goals in the 1951-52 season becoming the first non-British foreign player to become the top goalscorer in England. What was his nationality?

    a. Brazilian ☐

    b. Spanish ☐

    c. Chilean ☐

    d. Peruvian ☐

3. How many league goals did Newcastle score in the 1951-52 season in 42 matches?

    a. 75 ☐

    b. 79 ☐

    c. 89 ☐

    d. 98 ☐

4. Newcastle went back-to-back and won the FA cup again in the 1951-52 beating who 1-0 in the final?

    a. Arsenal ☐

    b. Sheffield Wednesday ☐

    c. Manchester United ☐

    d. Cardiff City ☐

5. Newcastle won another FA cup on 7 May 1955. Jackie Milburn opened the scoring in what was a record time. After how many seconds did he score?

    a. 12 ☐

    b. 25 ☐

    c. 45 ☐

    d. 58 ☐

6. Which player was top league goalscorer for Newcastle in each season between 1957 and 1961?

    a. Jackie Milburn ☐

    b. Len White ☐

    c. George Robledo ☐

    d. Tommy Walker ☐

7. Which former player was appointed Newcastle manager in 1962 - he remained until 1975 and oversaw 591 games as manager?

    a. Charlie Crowe ☐

    b. Frank Brennan ☐

    c. Joe Harvey ☐

    d. Hughie Gallacher ☐

8. What Fullback joined the club in 1962? He went on to make 457 appearances before leaving in 1975 to join Nottingham Forest who he also went on to manage.

   a. Stan Anderson ☐

   b. Joe Butler ☐

   c. Bobby Moncur ☐

   d. Frank Clark ☐

9. Newcastle had been relegated at the end of the 1960-1961 season. Promotion came after winning the second division in what season?

   a. 1962-63 ☐

   b. 1963-64 ☐

   c. 1964-65 ☐

   d. 1965-66 ☐

10. In 1969 Newcastle won the Inter-Cities Fairs Cup – who was their number 1 Goalkeeper at this time?

    a. David Hollins ☐

    b. Gordon Marshall ☐

    c. Martin Burleigh ☐

    d. Willie McFaul ☐

(ANSWERS CAN BE FOUND ON PAGE 79)

NEWCASTLE ENGLAND WORLD CUP PLAYERS

To date eleven players have been selected by England in a World Cup Squad whilst at the club. Can you name them all? (Initials and WC year given)

JM	Brazil 1950	
IB	Switzerland 1954	
PB	Mexico 1986	
AS	France 1998	
DB	France 1998	
RL	France 1998	
KD	Japan & Korea 2002	
MO	Germany 2006	
KT	Qatar 2022	
NP	Qatar 2022	
CW	Qatar 2022	

(ANSWERS CAN BE FOUND ON PAGE 80)

SECTION SEVEN

NEWCASTLE UNITED 1970s

1. Who finished as Newcastle's top goalscorer in the 1971/2, 72/73, 73/74 ad 74/75 season?

   a. John Tudor ☐

   b. Malcolm Macdonald ☐

   c. Bobby Moncur ☐

   d. Terry McDermott ☐

2. On 5 February 1972 Newcastle were knocked out in an FA cup 3rd round replay against which non-League club?

   a. Hayes & Yeading ☐

   b. Doncaster ☐

   c. Darlington ☐

   d. Hereford ☐

3. In 1974 a bad-tempered FA Cup quarter final match resulted in a ban from hosting home cup games in the following season. Who were their opponents that day?

    a. Tottenham Hotspur ☐

    b. Nottingham Forest ☐

    c. Sunderland ☐

    d. Chelsea ☐

4. Newcastle striker Malcolm Macdonald scored 5 goals for England on 16 April 1975 against which country?

    a. Cyprus ☐

    b. Bulgaria ☐

    c. Wales ☐

    d. Scotland ☐

5. Newcastle qualified for the UEFA cup following the 1976-77 season. They were knocked out in the second round against which French club?

    a. Auxerre ☐

    b. Lens ☐

    c. Marseille ☐

    d. Bastia ☐

6. Newcastle competed in the League Cup Final against which club in February 1976. Eventually losing 2-1 to which team?

    a. Manchester United ☐

    b. Manchester City ☐

    c. Liverpool ☐

    d. Leicester City ☐

7. On the 30th of January 1977 what manager left the club to join Everton?

    a. Gordon Lee ☐

    b. Richard Dinnis ☐

    c. Geoff Nulty ☐

    d. Norman Smith ☐

8. In December 1978 which Striker signed for the club from Blyth Spartans? He went on to score 38 goals in 117 games for the club.

    a. John Connolly ☐

    b. Peter Withe ☐

    c. Geoff Pike ☐

    d. Alan Shoulder ☐

9. A poor 1977-78 season saw Newcastle relegated to the second division with the lowest seasonal points haul in their history. How many points did they amass?

    a. 15 ☐

    b. 20 ☐

    c. 22 ☐

    d. 28 ☐

10. Despite this low haul. They did not finish bottom of the league. Another team got the same number of points but had a worse goal difference. Which club was this?

    a. Queens Park Rangers ☐

    b. Bristol City ☐

    c. Ipswich Town ☐

    d. Leicester City ☐

(ANSWERS CAN BE FOUND ON PAGE 81)

SECTION EIGHT

CROSSING THE DIVIDE

Clues to three players that made over 100 appearances for both Newcastle and Sunderland.

1. Signed by Sunderland from Manchester City in 1975 this player then transferred to Newcastle in 1982 on a free transfer. This defender played 124 league games in 5 years at the club

2. A Sunderland midfield youth product who signed for Newcastle on a free transfer in 2014 where he remained until 2020 scoring 5 goals in 102 matches.

3. Starting his career at Sunderland in 1981 this defender transferred to Newcastle from Liverpool in 1992. He made 130 appearances for Newcastle before signing for Galatasaray for £750,000

Two managers also crossed the divide. They remain the only two men at present to manage both clubs. Can you name them both?

4. Appointed Newcastle manager in May 2007 after a successful spell at Bolton he managed just 24 games before being replaced by Kevin Keegan

5. Managed 97 games for Newcastle between 2019-2021. This manager was replaced permanently by Eddie Howe

(ANSWERS CAN BE FOUND ON PAGE 82)

NEWCASTLE UNITED 1980s

1. In July 1980 Newcastle signed a 19-year-old for £10,000. He played 170 league games and scored 46 goals before joining Tottenham Hotspur for £590,000. Can you name him?

    a. Glenn Hoddle ☐

    b. Mick Harford ☐

    c. Chris Waddle ☐

    d. Peter Beardsley ☐

2. Signed from Southampton for a fee of £100,000 in 1982 this twice European player of the year won Newcastle's player of the year in 1982/3 and 1983/4 season. Who is he?

    a. Terry McDermott ☐

    b. Kevin Keegan ☐

    c. Mick Channon ☐

    d. Jeff Clarke ☐

3. In 1982 who recorded "Going home: Theme of the Local hero" that became synonymous with Newcastle united

   a. Sting ☐

   b. Jimmy Nail ☐

   c. George Michael ☐

   d. Mark Knopfler ☐

4. Making his debut in 1985 and playing 104 games for the club scoring 25 goals this generational talent left the club to join Tottenham Hotspur in 1988. Who is he?

   a. Peter Beardsley ☐

   b. Glenn Hoddle ☐

   c. Paul Gascoigne ☐

   d. Mick Quinn ☐

5. Who was the clubs top goalscorer in the 1984/5 and 1985/6?

   a. Paul Goddard ☐

   b. Mick Channon ☐

   c. Kevin Keegan ☐

   d. Peter Beardsley ☐

6. Which former player was appointed manager in September 1985? He remained until 1988 overseeing 140 games winning 47 of them.

    a. Willie McFaul ☐

    b. John Tudor ☐

    c. Malcolm Macdonald ☐

    d. Bobby Moncur ☐

7. In 1987 Newcastle signed the first ever Brazilian to play in England. Who was he?

    a. Josimar ☐

    b. Socrates ☐

    c. Mirandinha ☐

    d. Branco ☐

8. A new manager was appointed in December 1988 when he left QPR to join the club. Following relegation in 1989 he left Newcastle whilst they were in the second division in 1991

    a. Ossie Ardiles ☐

    b. Jim Smith ☐

    c. Dave Bassett ☐

    d. Steve Coppell ☐

9. Newcastle finished 3rd in the 1989/90 season meaning they were left in the play-off positions. After drawing 0-0 in the first leg they were knocked out after losing 2-0 in the home leg against which club?

   a. Sunderland ☐

   b. West Ham United ☐

   c. Swindon Town ☐

   d. Blackburn Rovers ☐

10. Despite the disappointment of not gaining promotion a Newcastle striker finished the season as the league's top goalscorer with 32 goals. Can you name him?

   a. Mick Channon ☐

   b. Mark McGhee ☐

   c. Mick Quinn ☐

   d. David Kelly ☐

(ANSWERS CAN BE FOUND ON PAGE 83)

YOUTH MAGPIES

Initials	League Games	Years	Name
1. AH	205	97-05	
2. SW	208	90-98	
3. SA	312	00-14	
4. AC	117	06-21*	
5. TK	160	06-17	
6. ST	215	03-16	
7. SH	191	89-00	
8. LC	217	90-97	
9. PB	276	83-97*	
10. PD	191	2010-	
11. RE	132	91-97	

Above are Clues to Newcastle youth products with over 100 appearances for the club - his initials, number of league games for the club and the years he played for the club are provided (*across two spells)

(ANSWERS CAN BE FOUND ON PAGE 84)

SECTION ELEVEN

NEWCASTLE UNITED 1990s

1. Making his debut at just 16 years and 223 days old in November 1990 against Wolves. Who to date remains the youngest player to represent the club?

    a. Steve Watson ☐

    b. Lee Clark ☐

    c. Gavin Peacock ☐

    d. Robbie Elliot ☐

2. In 1991 Newcastle signed a goalkeeper for £350,000 - he represented the Czech Republic 49 times. Can you name him?

    a. David Rozenhal ☐

    b. Martin Dubravka ☐

    c. Pavel Srnicek ☐

    d. Michel Travnik ☐

3. With Newcastle perilously close to relegation to the third tier of English football who was appointed as manager in February 1992 to save the club?

   a. Dave Bassett ☐

   b. Ossie Ardiles ☐

   c. Terry McDermott ☐

   d. Kevin Keegan ☐

4. Newcastle turned their fortunes around and were promoted as winners of the second tier in the 1992/93 season – who was the clubs top goalscorer that season with 28 goals?

   a. Micky Quinn ☐

   b. David Kelly ☐

   c. Gavin Peacock ☐

   d. Andy Hunt ☐

5. In the now newly formed Premier League what Newcastle striker scored 41 goals in the 1993/94 season with 34 coming in the league?

    a. Alan Shearer ☐

    b. Gavin Peacock ☐

    c. Andy Cole ☐

    d. Teddy Sheringham ☐

6. Signed in the summer of 1995 for £6 million who scored 29 goals in his debut season?

    a. Darren Huckerby ☐

    b. Paul Kitson ☐

    c. Malcolm Allen ☐

    d. Les Ferdinand ☐

7. What Frenchman signed for the club for a fee of £2.5 million in 1995? he scored 7 goals in his time with the club.

    a. David Ginola ☐

    b. Phillipe Albert ☐

    c. David Terrier ☐

    d. Louis Saha ☐

8. Alan Shearer scored his first goal for the club on 21st August 1996. A stunning free kick in a 2-0 win. Who were the opponents that day?

    a. Leicester City ☐

    b. Wimbledon ☐

    c. Southampton ☐

    d. Manchester United ☐

9. Arriving on Tyneside in the snow in 1996. Which Colombian joined the club scoring 18 goals in 61 games before rejoining Parma?

    a. Shaka Hislop ☐

    b. Rodney Jack ☐

    c. Nolberto Solano ☐

    d. Faustino Asprilla ☐

10. Sir Bobby Robsons first game in charge on September 19th 1999 resulted in an 8-0 win against which club?

    a. Sheffield Wednesday ☐

    b. Leeds United ☐

    c. Swindon Town ☐

    d. Charlton Athletic ☐

(ANSWERS CAN BE FOUND ON PAGE 85)

SECTION TWELVE

NEWCASTLE UNITED 1999 FA CUP FINAL XI

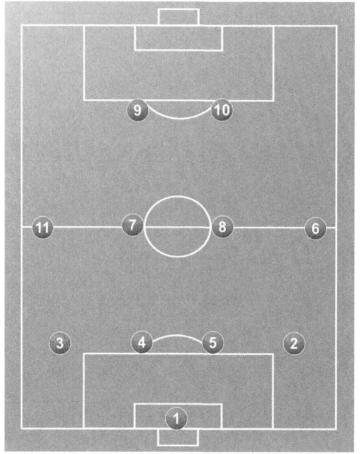

(The numbers used are to represent positions only – they are not accurate as worn on the day)

How many of the Newcastle United 1999 FA CUP XI final can you name?

1. SH	
2. AG	
3. DD	
4. ND	
5. LC	
6. DH	
7. GS	
8. RL	
9. AS	
10. TK	
11. NS	

(ANSWERS CAN BE FOUND ON PAGE 86)

SECTION THIRTEEN

NEWCASTLE UNITED 2000s

1. In 2002 Rob Lee left the club after 10 years and 381 games for the club. Who did he sign from 10 years earlier?

    a. West Ham United ☐

    b. Portsmouth ☐

    c. Charlton Athletic ☐

    d. Queens Park Rangers ☐

2. What defender signed for Real Madrid in 2004? He had an injury plagued time with Newcastle.

    a. Alessandro Pistonc ☐

    b. Jonathan Woodgate ☐

    c. Sylvain Distin ☐

    d. Aaron Hughes ☐

3. Departing the club in 2004 for Bolton. What versatile leader scored 40 goals in 285 games after signing from Everton for £5.5 million in 1998.

    a. Rob Lee ☐

    b. Lee Bowyer ☐

    c. Kieron Dyer ☐

    d. Gary Speed ☐

4. In the 2004/05 season. Alan Shearer scored his last European goals in the UEFA cup. He is Newcastle's top goalscorer in all European competitions. How many goals did he score?

    a. 18 ☐

    b. 25 ☐

    c. 30 ☐

    d. 38 ☐

5. Lee Bowyer and Kieran Dyer were involved in an infamous on field bust up in April 2005 which saw both players sent off. Who were the opponents that day?

    a. Manchester United ☐

    b. Sunderland ☐

    c. Aston Villa ☐

    d. Birmingham City ☐

6. Newcastle signed this hardworking midfielder from Chelsea in 2005. He played 73 games for the club in two seasons before leaving to join West Ham United. Can you name him?

    a. Scott Parker ☐

    b. Rob Lee ☐

    c. Nolberto Solano ☐

    d. Craig Bellamy ☐

7. Alan Shearer dominated the Newcastle top goalscorer spot for five seasons. In 2006/07 season there was a new top goalscorer. Who scored 17 goals in the 2006/07 season?

    a. Obafemi Martins ☐

    b. Carl Cort ☐

    c. Shola Ameobi ☐

    d. Patrick Kluivert ☐

8. In 2006 Newcastle signed an Irish winger from Chelsea for a fee of £5 million. He stayed at the club until 2009 making 86 appearances.

    a. Stephen Carr ☐

    b. Leon Best ☐

    c. Aiden McGeady ☐

    d. Damien Duff ☐

9. Which Argentinian made their debut for Newcastle United against Manchester United in August 2008 alongside fellow newly signed Argentinian Fabricio Coloccini?

   a. Nacho Gonzalez ☐

   b. Javier Mascherano ☐

   c. Jonas Gutierrez ☐

   d. Maxi Rodriguez ☐

10. A former Manchester United player was appointed Newcastle club captain for the 2009/10 season. He played 173 games for Newcastle scoring 5 goals.

   a. Michael Owen ☐

   b. Nicky Butt ☐

   c. Alan Smith ☐

   d. Joey Barton ☐

(ANSWERS CAN BE FOUND ON PAGE 87)

NEWCASTLE UNITED 2009/10 PROMOTION BEST XI

This XI appeared the most times this season:

1. SH	45 GAMES	
2. FC	37 GAMES	
3. JE	33 GAMES	
4. ST	21 GAMES	
5. DS	39 GAMES	
6. KN	44 GAMES	
7. DG	36 GAMES	
8. AS	31 GAMES	
9. JG	34 GAMES	
10. AC	33 GAMES	
11. PL	19 GAMES	

Also, this defender played a vital role

12. RT	19 GAMES	

(ANSWERS CAN BE FOUND ON PAGE 88)

SECTION FIFTEEN

NEWCASTLE UNITED 2010s

1. Newcastle gained promotion back to the Premier League in the 2009/10 season. Who finished top goalscorer with 19 goals?

   a. Kevin Nolan ☐

   b. Alan Smith ☐

   c. Peter Lovenkrands ☐

   d. Andy Carroll ☐

2. Back in the Premier League Newcastle finished 12th. What midfielder was top goalscorer with 12 goals this season?

    a. Jonas Gutierrez ☐

    b. Kevin Nolan ☐

    c. Joey Barton ☐

    d. Danny Guthrie ☐

3. Andy Carroll left the club to join Liverpool in 2011 for a club record selling fee. How much did he go for?

    a. £15 million ☐

    b. £25 million ☐

    c. £35 million ☐

    d. £45 million ☐

4. Who scored 13 goals in just 14 matches during the 2011-12 season after signing in January 2012?

    a. Papiss Cisse ☐

    b. Demba Ba ☐

    c. Hatem Ben Arfa ☐

    d. Shola Ameobi ☐

5. Scoring against Metalist Kharvik on 21st February 2013 what player became the clubs second highest goalscorer in European competitions (behind Shearer) with 15 goals

    a. Kevin Nolan ☐

    b. Shola Ameobi ☐

    c. Papiss Cisse ☐

    d. Yoan Gouffran ☐

6. Signing for a fee of £20 million from PSV which Dutch midfielder joined the club on 11ᵗʰ July 2015?

    a. Daryl Janmaat ☐

    b. Siem De Jong ☐

    c. Vernon Anita ☐

    d. Gini Wijnaldum ☐

7. On 11ᵗʰ March what manager was brought to the club to replace Steve McClaren? He achieved a 42.5% win rate in 146 games as manager

    a. Alan Pardew ☐

    b. Steve Bruce ☐

    c. Rafael Benitez ☐

    d. Alan Pardew ☐

8. Despite this appointment Newcastle were relegated at the end of the season. However, on May 15th they produced a stunning display beating which club 5-1?

   a. Manchester City ☐

   b. Tottenham Hotspur ☐

   c. Arsenal ☐

   d. Manchester United ☐

9. Newcastle gained automatic promotion back to the Premier League at the first time of asking in the 2016/17 season. What player signed for the club on 1st July 2016 and top scored with 23 league goals this season?

   a. Cheick Tiote ☐

   b. Aleksander Mitrovic ☐

   c. Daryl Murphy ☐

   d. Dwight Gayle ☐

10. After gaining promotion back to the Premier League what position did Newcastle finish in the 2017/18 season?

    a. 5th ☐

    b. 10th ☐

    c. 15th ☐

    d. 18th ☐

(ANSWERS CAN BE FOUND ON PAGE 89)

SECTION SIXTEEN

NEWCASTLE UNITED
2016/17 PROMOTION TEAM THAT
BEAT QPR 6-0 AWAY FROM HOME

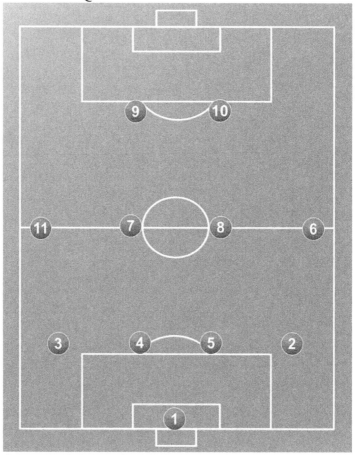

(The numbers used are to represent positions only – they are not accurate as worn on the day)

Newcastle United team that beat QPR 6-0 away from home during the 2016/17 promotion season

1. MS	
2. CC	
3. PD	
4. JL	
5. VA	
6. MR	
7. JS	
8. IH	
9. AP	
10. YG	
11. AM	

(ANSWERS CAN BE FOUND ON PAGE (90)

NEWCASTLE UNITED 2020s

1. On 7th September 2020 which striker did Newcastle sign from Bournemouth for a fee of £20,000,000?

   a. Jamal Lewis ☐

   b. Callum Wilson ☐

   c. Chris Wood ☐

   d. Joe Willock ☐

2. What club did Newcastle beat 7-0 in the EFL cup third round in September 2020?

   a. Macclesfield Town ☐

   b. Exeter City ☐

   c. Morecambe ☐

   d. Millwall ☐

3. Newcastle signed which player on loan right at the end of the January transfer window? He eventually signed permanently from Arsenal for a fee of £25,000,000

   a. Joe Willock ☐

   b. Matt Targett ☐

   c. Jeff Hendrick ☐

   d. Ryan Fraser ☐

4. In what month of 2021 did Mike Ashley relinquish control of the club to the Public Investment Fund?

   a. February ☐

   b. June ☐

   c. July ☐

   d. October ☐

5. Who was appointed manager of Newcastle on 8th November 2021?

   a. Alan Pardew ☐

   b. Eddie Howe ☐

   c. Steve Bruce ☐

   d. David Moyes ☐

6. Following the Public Investment Fund takeover, who was the clubs first major signing on 7th January 2021?

    a. Kieran Trippier ☐

    b. Ryan Fraser ☐

    c. Dan Burn ☐

    d. Joelinton ☐

7. Signed in January 2022 from Lyon – which player became Newcastles record transfer who joined for £40 million?

    a. Chris Wood ☐

    b. Sven Botman ☐

    c. Aleksander Isak ☐

    d. Bruno Guimaraes ☐

8. Newcastle have had 19 managers since Bobby Robson departed in 2004. Which manager has overseen the most games during his tenure (185)?

    a. Sam Allardyce ☐

    b. Alan Pardew ☐

    c. Rafael Benitez ☐

    d. Graeme Souness ☐

9. And which manager has the highest % win rate during a spell at the club with 59% he was manager for 64 games winning 38 of them

    a. Steve McClaren ☐

    b. Steve Bruce ☐

    c. John Carver ☐

    d. Chris Hughton ☐

10. Who was Newcastles number 1 at the start of the 2022/23 season?

    a. Martin Dubravka ☐

    b. Nick Pope ☐

    c. Karl Darlow ☐

    d. Loris Karius ☐

(ANSWERS CAN BE FOUND ON PAGE 91)

ANSWERS

Section one: Early History of Newcastle United

1. B – Newcastle East End

2. A – Woolwich Arsenal

3. C – 13TH

4. D – 1904-1905

5. C - 3

6. C – Frank Watt

7. D – Jimmy Lawrence

8. B - Barnsley

9. C – Albert Shepherd

10. A – Bradford City

/10

ANSWERS

Section two: Name the famous Magpie

1. Andy Cole

2. John Anderson

3. Jackie Milburn

4. Peter Beardlsey

5. Terry McDermott

6. Nolberto Solano

7. Bryan Robson

8. Malcolm McDonald

9. Demba Ba

10. Shay Given

/10

ANSWERS

Section Three: Newcastle 1974 FA CUP FINAL XI

1. IM   Ian McFaul

2. FC   Frank Clark

3. AK   Alan Kennedy

4. TM   Terry McDermott

5. PH   Pat Howard

6. BM   Bobby Moncur

7. JS   Jim Smith

8. TC   Thomas Cassidy

9. MM   Malcolm MacDonald

10. JT   John Tudor

11. TH   Terry Hibbitt

12. TG   Thomas Gibb

/12

ANSWERS

Section four: Newcastle United 1920s-1940s

1. A – Aston Villa

2. B - Everton

3. C – Hughie Gallacher

4. B - Chelsea

5. B – The ball went out of play

6. C – 1933-34

7. A – Stan Seymour

8. C – 13-0

9. D – Len Shackleton

10. D – Birmingham City

/10

ANSWERS

Section Five: Newcastle United 1950s-1960s

1. D – Jackie Milburn

2. C – Chilean

3. D – 98

4. A - Arsenal

5. C – 45 seconds

6. B – Len White

7. C – Joe Harvey

8. D – Frank Clark

9. C – 1964-65

10. D – Willie McFaul

/10

ANSWERS

Section six: Newcastle World Cup England Players

1. JM – Jackie Milburn

2. IB – Ivan Broadis

3. PB – Peter Beardsley

4. AS – Alan Shearer

5. DB – David Batty

6. RL – Rob Lee

7. KD – Kieran Dyer

8. MO – Michael Owen

9. KT – Kieran Trippier

10. NP – Nick Pope

11. CW – Callum Wilson

/10

ANSWERS

Section seven: Newcastle United 1970s

1. B – Malcolm Macdonald

2. D – Hereford

3. B – Nottingham Forest

4. A – Cyprus

5. D – Bastia

6. B – Manchester City

7. A – Gordon Lee

8. D – Alan Shoulder

9. C – 22 points

10. D – Leicester City

/10

ANSWERS

Section eight: Crossing the Divide

1. Jeff Clarke

2. Jack Colback

3. Pop Robson

4. Barry Venison

5. Sam Allardyce

6. Steve Bruce

/6

ANSWERS

Section nine: Newcastle United 1980s

1. C – Chris Waddle

2. B – Kevin Keegan

3. D – Mark Knopfler

4. C – Paul Gascoigne

5. D – Peter Beardsley

6. A – Willie McFaul

7. C – Mirandinha

8. B – Jim Smith

9. A – Sunderland

10. C – Mick Quinn

/10

ANSWERS

Section Ten: Young Magpies

1. Aaron Hughes

2. Steve Watson

3. Shola Ameobi

4. Andy Carroll

5. Tim Krul

6. Steven Taylor

7. Steve Howey

8. Lee Clark

9. Peter Beardsley

10. Paul Dummett

11. Robbie Elliot

/11

ANSWERS

Section Eleven: Newcastle United 1990s

1. A – Steve Watson

2. C – Pavel Srnicek

3. D – Kevin Keegan

4. B – David Kelly

5. C – Andy Cole

6. D – Les Ferdinand

7. A – David Ginola

8. B – Wimbledon

9. D – Faustino Asprilla

10. A – Sheffield Wednesday

/10

ANSWERS

Section Twelve: Newcastle United 1999 FA CUP final XI

1. SH	Steve Harper
2. AG	Andy Griffin
3. DD	Didier Domi
4. ND	Nikos Dabizas
5. LC	Laurent Charvet
6. DH	Dietmar Hamann
7. GS	Gary Speed
8. RL	Rob Lee
9. AS	Alan Shearer
10. TK	Temuri Ketsbaia
11. NS	Nolberto Solano

/11

ANSWERS

Section Thirteen: Newcastle United 2000s

1. C – Charlton Athletic

2. B – Jonathan Woodgate

3. D – Gary Speed

4. C – 30

5. C – Aston Villa

6. A – Scott Parker

7. A – Obafemi Martins

8. D – Damien Duff

9. C – Jonas Gutierrez

10. B – Nicky Butt

/10

ANSWERS

Section Fourteen: Newcastle United Promotion XI

1. SH	Steve Harper
2. FC	Fabricio Collocini
3. JE	Jose Enrique
4. ST	Steve Taylor
5. DS	Danny Simpson
6. KN	Kevin Nolan
7. DG	Danny Guthrie
8. AS	Alan Smith
9. JG	James Gutierrez
10. AC	Andy Carroll
11. PL	Peter Lovenkrands
12. RT	Ryan Taylor

/12

ANSWERS

Section Fifteen: Newcastle United 2010s

1. D – Andy Carroll

2. B – Kevin Nolan

3. C - £35 million

4. A – Papiss Cisse

5. B – Shola Ameobi

6. D – Gini Wijnaldum

7. C – Rafa Benitez

8. B – Tottenham Hotspur

9. D – Dwight Gayle

10. B – 10th

/10

ANSWERS

Section Sixteen: Newcastle United 6-0 winners over QPR

1. Matz Sels
2. Ciaran Clark
3. Paul Dummett
4. Jamaal Lascelles
5. Vurnon Anita
6. Matt Ritchie
7. Jonjo Shelvey
8. Isaac Hayden
9. Ayoze Perez
10. Yoan Gouffran
11. Aleksander Mitrovic

/11

ANSWERS

Section Seventeen: Newcastle United 2020s

1. B – Callum Wilson

2. C – Morecambe

3. A – Joe Willock

4. D – October 2021

5. B – Eddie Howe

6. A – Kieran Trippier

7. D – Bruno Guimaraes

8. B – Alan Pardew

9. D – Chris Hughton

10. B – Nick Pope

/10

That completes the quiz and with a total of 173 points available – where do you stand?

150-173 True Toon

125-149 Magic Magpie

101-124 North East and Proud

51-100 Room for Improvement

26-50 Still learning the ropes

0-25 Are you a Mackem in disguise???

Hopefully you have enjoyed this little quiz book and it has been a challenge but your knowledge has extended and been rewarded. Now it's time to challenge your friends and family. Challenge the ardent fan that claims they know everything and see whether they are a True Toon or a closet Mackem,

Take away multiple choice options for the easier questions and use the book to teach the next generation of fans about the history of our great club.

Printed in Great Britain
by Amazon

33791558R00057